QUILT DESIGNS
COLORING BOOK
FOR ADULTS

36 Vintage Full Quilt Coloring Pages

Plus

78 Named Quilt Blocks

to

Embellish and Color

the Green-Eyed-Lady
Books.SmartSeniorpreneur.com

Tips for Best Results

Hello, I'm so glad you're here.

Maybe you're like me...

I've been enchanted by hand-made quilts since my grandmother made one just for me, sixty years ago. I still remember some of my own old hand-me-down dresses, blouses and skirts that she used for the colorful patches that made up that gorgeous double wedding-ring design!

This book contains many pieced patchwork designs -- complete quilts as well as single blocks, along with a few appliqué patterns for your coloring enjoyment.

As you color, I hope you can imagine pioneer women piecing together precious scraps of fabric and embellishing their finished quilts with fanciful stitching -- busy work for long evenings that helped wash away the stress of new settlers' daily lives.

Today, you can wash away the stress of modern life by coloring and embellishing these pages - no sewing required.

MEDIA

A good set of coloring pencils and a sharpener are essential!

Although gel pens and markers can add bright pops of color to your designs, be careful and test first – they may bleed through. There's a test page of patches at the back of the book for that purpose.

Since we have no control over paper quality with Amazon-published books, it's important to place a sheet of heavy paper or even a piece of cereal-box cardboard behind the page you're working on to keep from marring pages beneath.

Use the test page to practice blending and layering colors for different effects, too.

EMBELLISHMENT

Color the "patches" as solid colors or add your own stripes, plaids, or simulated patterned fabrics. Try out your ideas on the test page at the back of the book!

Since the actual quilting is an integral part of real quilts, try adding your own simulated stitching patterns with pencil or Fineliner™ pen. (Experiment with different "thread" colors)

You can simulate the simplest of designs by making a dashed line just inside a patch shape or in a grid pattern over the entire quilt — or you can add cross-stitching or blanket stitches or any other favorite quilting or embroidery technique you like.

Take advantage of blank sash and/or borders to add fanciful swirls, scallops, waves, feathers, and garlands. Let your imagination soar! You may want to "audition" your ideas by drawing them first on thin paper or tracing paper over the quilt design.

NAMES

Although each block and quilt is named, I've found that the same or similar designs appear under different names. As patterns were shared with family and friends as simple sketches, names seemed to morph with each share. What I know as "Ohio Star" might be a pattern YOU recognize as something different.

The coloring of a pattern makes a difference, too. The block labeled "Balkan Puzzle" would be called that if three colors were used – but if you color it with just two colors (or one + white) then it would be known as "Whirlpool". Another arrangement of colors for this pattern is called "Windblown Square". Same layout but completely different appearance.

ENJOY

This is YOUR book so do whatever you want with it. If you're left handed, you may find it easier to turn the book sideways with the spine at the top, or turn it upside down to color.

Don't be afraid to press down on the open pages so the book stays open to the page you want to work on.

Or, cut out the pages to work on them independently if you wish.

I hope you'll enjoy hours of relaxation and remembering simpler times as you color and embellish these pages.

REVIEW

If you liked this coloring book, I hope you'll take a moment to leave a review and tell others how much you enjoyed it. Please visit my website at Books.SmartSeniorPreneur.com and sign up for free printable coloring pages as well as news about upcoming new publications.

THANK YOU!

the Green-Eyed-Lady

Fifty-Four Forty or Fight

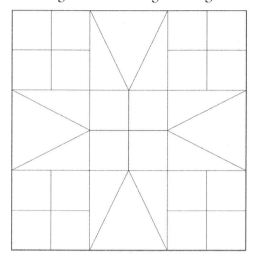

Aunt Malvina's Chain

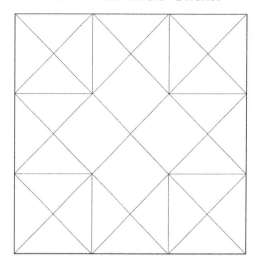

Handy Andy

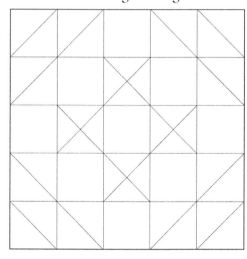

Corn and Beans

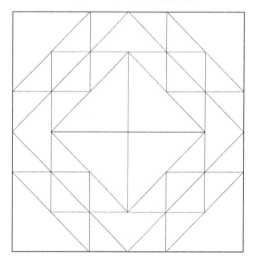

Star and Chains

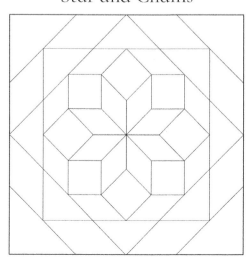

Road to California

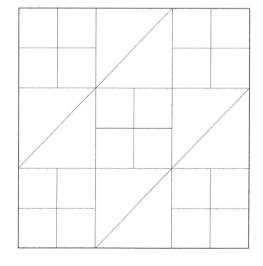

Fifty-Four-Forty or Fight & Aunt Malvina's Chain

Handy Andy

Log Cabin

Flying Fist

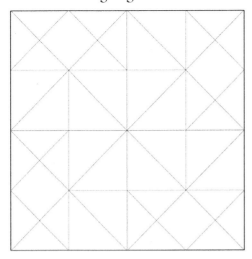

Buckwheat

Road to Oklahoma

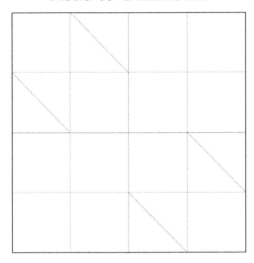

Cut Glass Dish

Storm at Sea

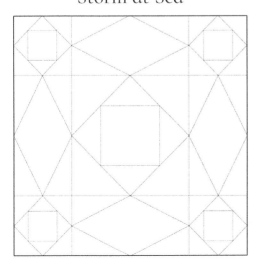

Bird's Nest

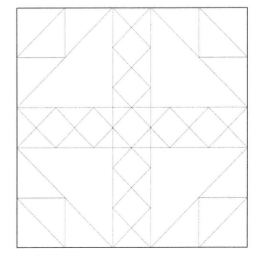

Buckwheat & Shoo Fly

Storm at Sea

Tulip Basket Appliqué

Cross and Crown

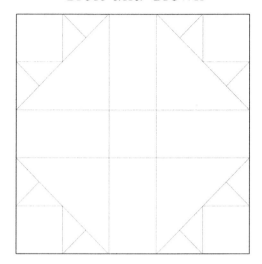

Blazing Star

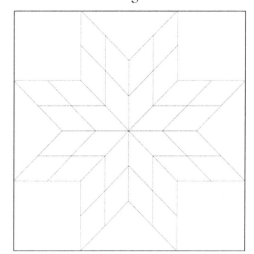

Susanna

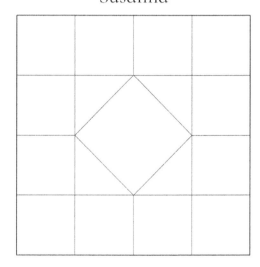

Dutchman's Puzzle

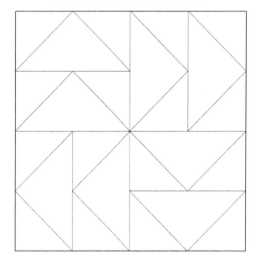

Old Maid's Puzzle

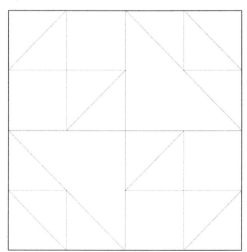

Time and Tide

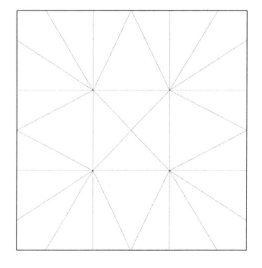

Susanna & Dutchman's Puzzle

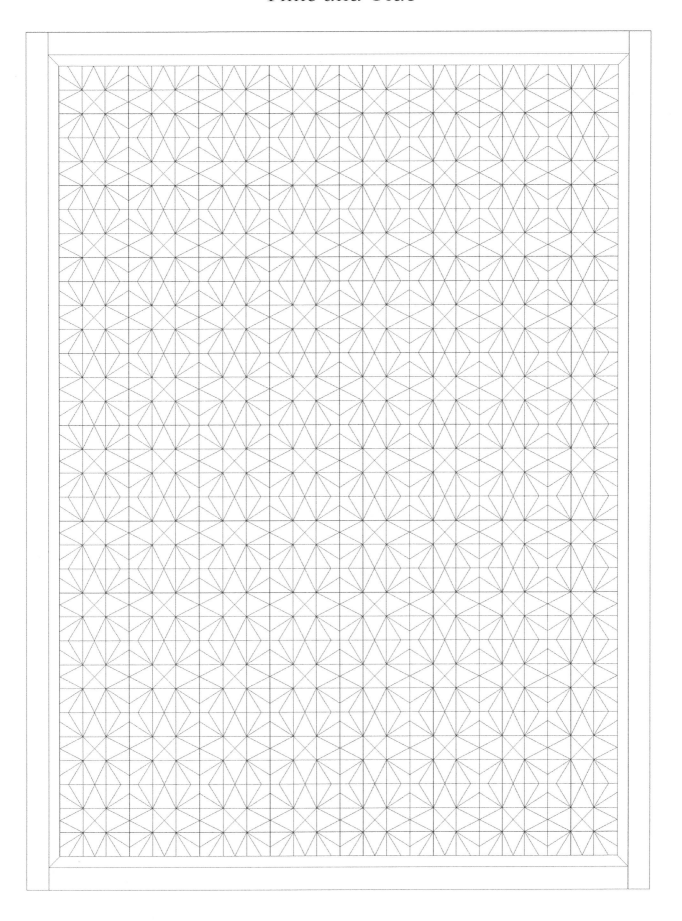

Dresden Fans

Alabama Beauty

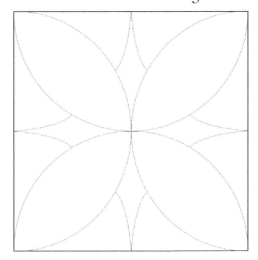

Mosaic #13

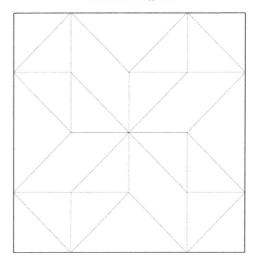

Children's Delight

Double X No. 4

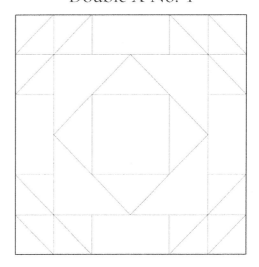

Bear's Paw

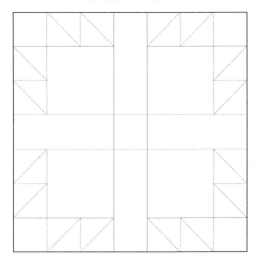

Flagstones

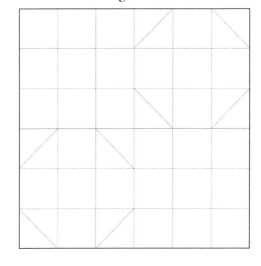

Alabama Beauty & Mosaic #13

Children's Delight

Feathered Star

Lover's Knot

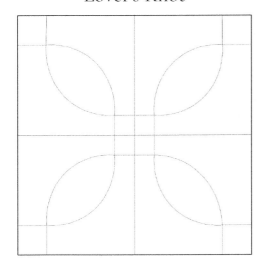

Chain

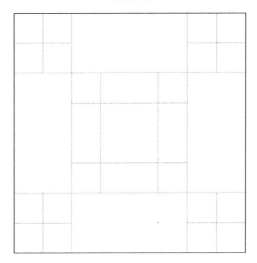

Basket Pinwheel

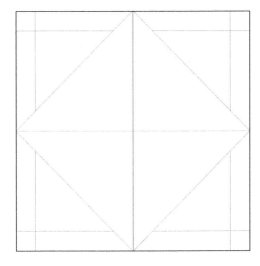

Pinwheel Circle

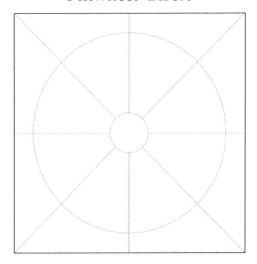

Melon Patch

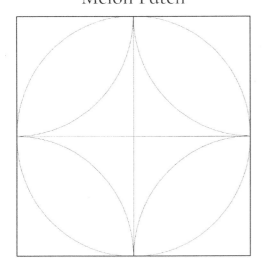

Johnnie-Round-the-Corner

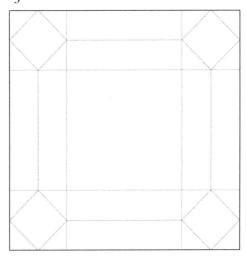

Lover's Knot & Chain

Pinwheel Circle & Basket Pinwheel

Sunbonnet Sue & Sam

Card Trick

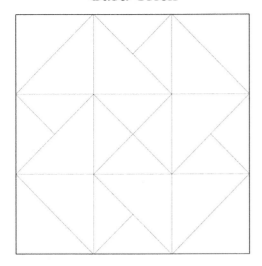

Nine-Patch Chain

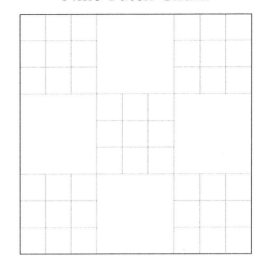

Balkan Puzzle

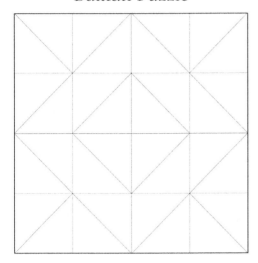

Kansas Troubles

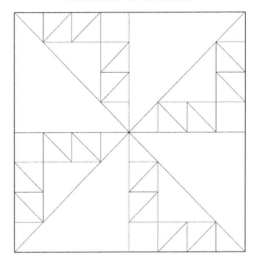

Clay's Choice

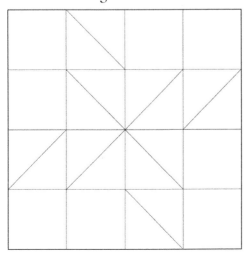

Greek Square

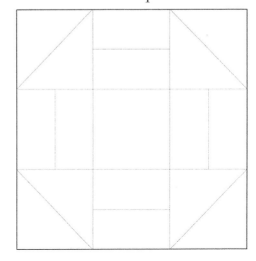

Card Trick

Balkan Puzzle

Dresden Plates & Nine-Patch Chains

Propeller

Winding Ways

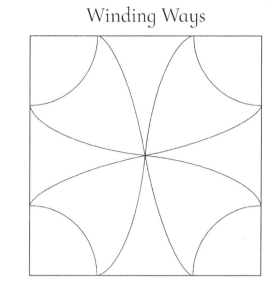

Beggar's Block

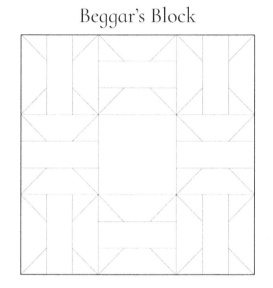

Domino

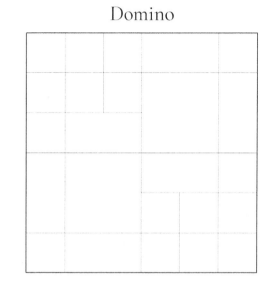

Pine Tree

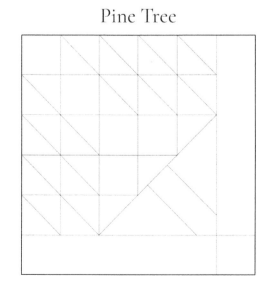

Indian Hatchets

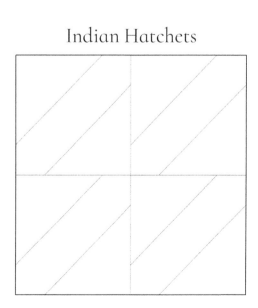

Propellers

Winding Ways

Double Wedding Ring

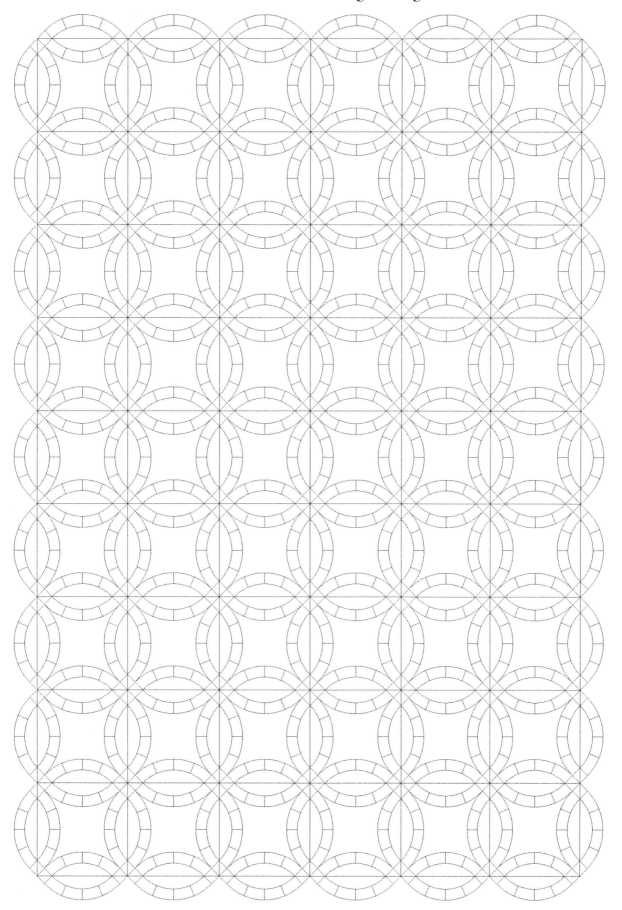

Weather Vane

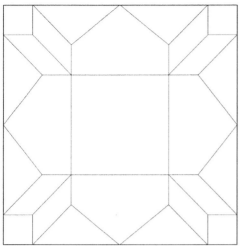

Lost Ship

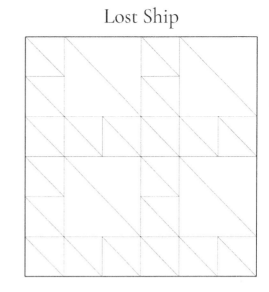

Hovering Hawks

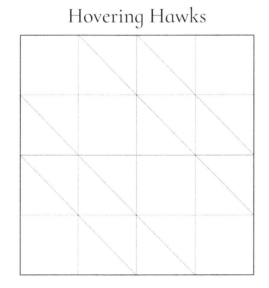

Hunter's Star

Leap Frog

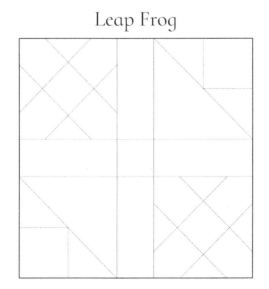

Whirligig

Hovering Hawks

Hunter's Stars

Baby Blocks

St. Louis Star

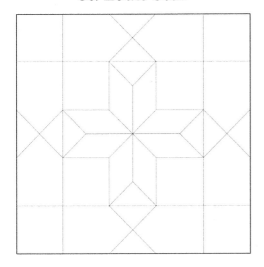

Hand Weave

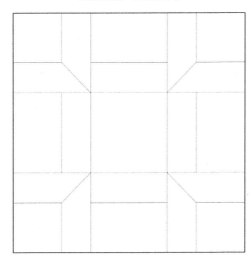

Merry Kite

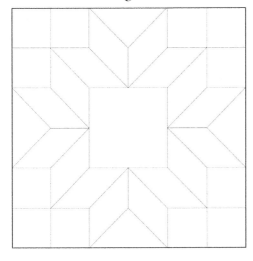

New York Beauty

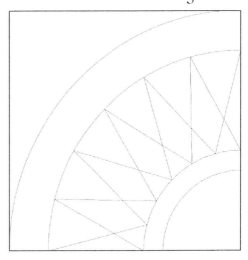

Cheyenne Star

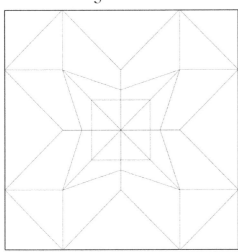

Steps to the Altar

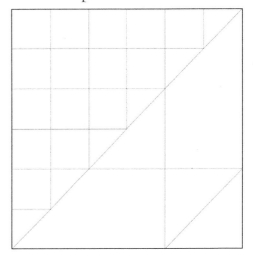

Hand Weave & St. Louis Star

Merry Kite

Butterflies & Flowers Appliqué

Savannah Star

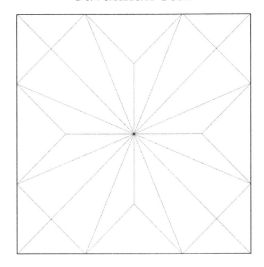

Star Wheel

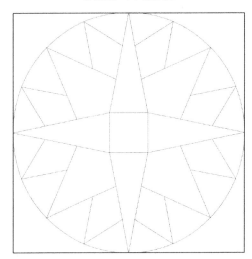

Cross Roads

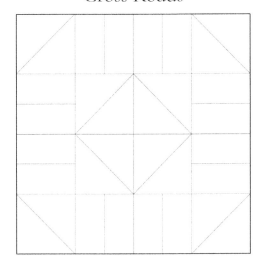

Rolling Crosses

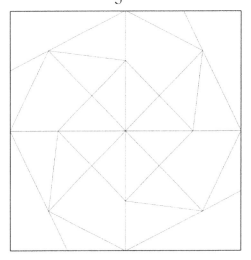

Wheel of Fortune

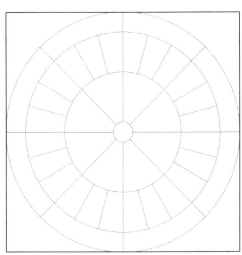

Texas Wheel

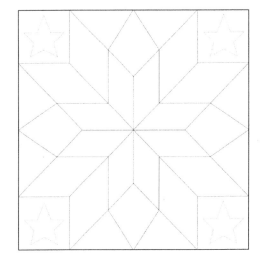

Savannah Star

Cross Roads & Rolling Crosses

Birds in the Air

Goose in the Pond

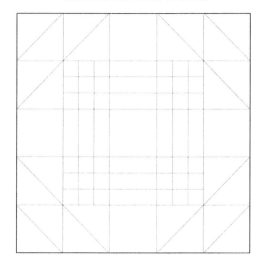

Drunkard's Path

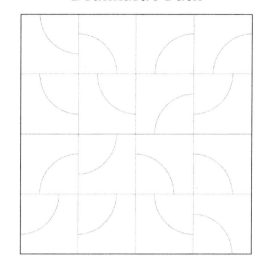

Sara's Favorite

Kansas Star

Mariner's Compass

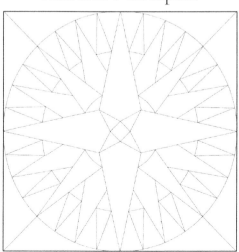

Chicago Star

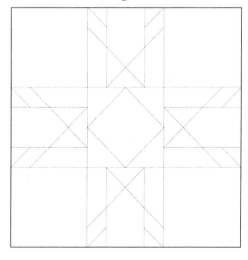

Chicago Star & Kansas Star

Drunkard's Path

Cobblestones

Crazy House

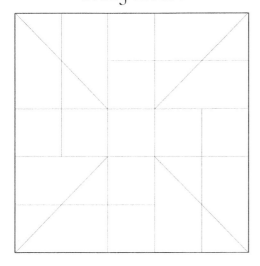

Widower's Choice

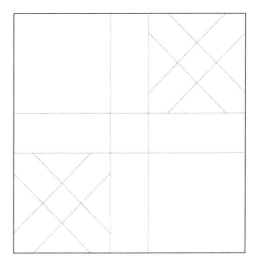

Mill Wheel

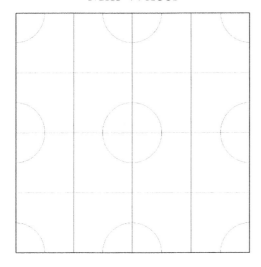

Sugar Bowl

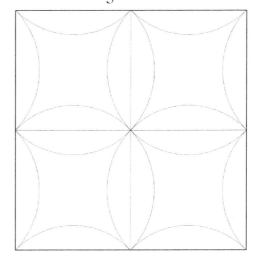

Texas Tears

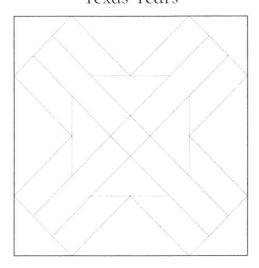

Star and Cubes

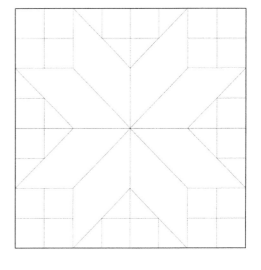

Mill Wheel

Sugar Bowl

Hour Glass & Letter X

Orange Peels

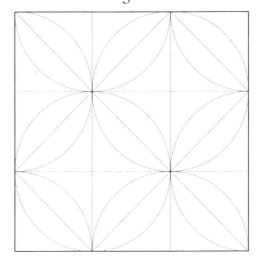

Shining Bright

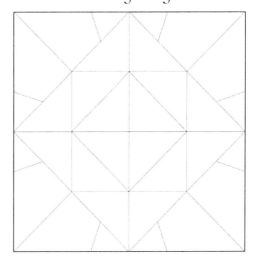

Flying Squares

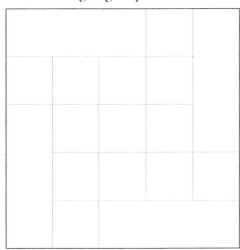

Pinwheel

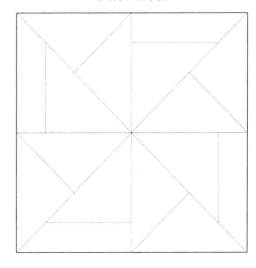

Ohio Star

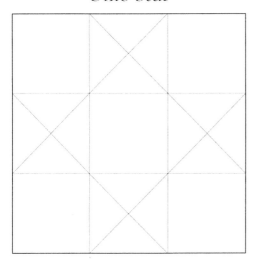

Barbershop Baskets

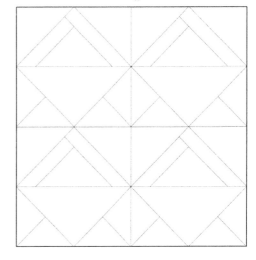

Test Page

Also Available from Green-Eyed Lady

Book #2 in the Quilt Designs Coloring Book series contains more old-time patchwork quilt blocks and quilts to color.

You'll also find an alphabetical visual index to the quilt blocks, shaded to give you an idea of how you might color each one.

Follow this link to purchase:

https://www.bklnk.com/process.php?q=B08WJTPVBW

or scan the code below with your phone's camera

Scan Me to Purchase...

Want to help others?

Could you do me a favor, please?

Hi, I'm the Green-Eyed Lady and creator of this coloring book.

If you enjoyed it, I'd really appreciate your taking 30 seconds to leave an **HONEST REVIEW** so others can benefit from your insights.

I don't have a big publishing house behind me that can spend thousands of dollars on marketing -- it's just me - a one-person home-based publishing business. So I depend very heavily on honest reviews from good people like you to help "get the word out" when my books are good (and/or give feedback on how I can improve them when they're not so good).

Believe it or not, I read all reviews personally. I really do care about what you have to say.

Thank you in advance!

To leave a review, just go to

www.amazon.com/review/create-review?&asin=**B08JDTRJ3B**

or scan the image below with your phone camera.

Get Free Printable Quilt Coloring Pages

Go to **books.smartseniorpreneur.com** to sign up for free printable coloring pages and be the first to hear about new releases!

Made in the USA
Coppell, TX
20 December 2024

42496627R00059